Byron Harmon

Mountain
Photographer

Byron Harmon

Mountain Photographer

Edited by Carole Harmon
Introductory Essay by Bart Robinson

Altitude Publishing

Banff Alberta Canada

1992

Halftitle page:

PACK TRAIN IN WILCOX PASS, YELLOWHEAD EXPEDITION, 1911

In 1911 the Athabasca Glacier filled the valley where the highway and the Icefield Chalet are today, and the gorge of the Sunwapta River, north of the Columbia Icefield, was filled with a rockslide. Parties bypassed the Columbia Icefield using Wilcox Pass in the next valley.

Frontispiece:

BYRON HARMON AT FORTRESS LAKE, 1924

This portrait of Byron Harmon with his motion picture camera was taken in 1924 by Lewis Freeman during the Columbia Icefield Expedition.

Front Cover:

TEEPEE AT BOW LAKE, COLUMBIA ICEFIELD EXPEDITION, 1924

Back Cover:

THE SUMMIT OF MT. RESPLENDENT, 1913

Canadian Cataloguing in Publication Data
Harmon, Byron, 1876-1942
Byron Harmon, mountain photographer
ISBN 0-919381-84-7
1. Harmon, Byron, 1876-1942.
2. Photography, Artistic.
3. Nature photography.
4. Rocky Mountains, Canadian (BC and Alta.) – Pictorial works.*
I. Harmon, Carole, 1947–
II. Title.
TR654.H37 1992   779'.092   C92-091706-2

All photographs in this book appear courtesy of the Whyte Museum of the Canadian Rockies.

This book was published with the assistance of the Alberta Foundation for the Literary Arts and Alberta Culture.

Editor: John F. Ricker

Design: Robert MacDonald, MediaClones

Printed by D. W. Friesen, Altona Manitoba

Back cover photograph hand-coloured by Carole Harmon

ALTITUDE PUBLISHING LTD.
Post Office Box 490
Banff Alberta Canada T0L 0C0

Printed in Canada

TO ORDER PHOTOGRAPHS FROM THIS BOOK:

Enlargements of the photographs in this book for research, reproduction, or general interest may be ordered from The Whyte Museum of the Canadian Rockies, POBox 160, Banff, Alberta, Canada T0L 0C0, (403) 762-2091. The museum also handles all research inquiries.

HANDMADE ART PRINTS:

Carole Harmon, granddaughter of Byron Harmon, is making handmade prints of a selection of images in this book on printing out paper, an antique handmade paper that was popular early in the century. Prints are contact printed and gold toned from specially produced enlarged negatives. The resulting prints have a tonal range and clarity that cannot be captured on modern enlarging papers. All prints are matted with archival matte board to 20"x 24". Prints of the following images may be ordered from: **Nature Works, PO Box 490, Banff, Alberta, Canada, T0L 0C0, (403) 762-8418.**

p. 20, A Native Chief
p. 41, Mt. Robson from the east, 1911 or 1913
p. 44 (bottom), Packtrain on upper Sunwapta River, 1911
p. 45, John Hunter preparing for the Sun Dance
p. 59 (top), Byron Harmon at a glacial lake in the Selkirk Range
p. 60, Byron Harmon with his movie camera overlooking Illicillewaet Valley
p. 61, Climbers on a moraine near Yoho Glacier, 1914
p. 72, The Lake of the Hanging Glaciers, 1922
p. 73 (bottom), Ice cave in Starbird Glacier, 1922
p. 79, Canoeing on the Cross River, 1923
p. 82, Bow Lake, 1924
p. 89, Mt. Quincy, 1924
p. 90, Mt. Columbia, 1924
p. 92, Ascending the divide between Poboktan and Jonas creeks, 1924
p. 104, Mt. Assiniboine, 1927

BART ROBINSON

A BIOGRAPHICAL PORTRAIT OF BYRON HARMON

When a 27-year-old itinerant photographer named Byron Harmon left a Canadian Pacific Railway coach at Banff, Northwest Territories, in 1903, he stepped into the right place at the right time.

He also stepped into a spot of extreme contrasts: a small, rough-hewn village, in the midst of a desolate mountain wilderness, which sported five first-class hotels and as bizarre an assortment of people as could be imagined. Pack-train outfitters in soiled chaps and beaten wide-brimmed hats, stocky European alpinists in knickers and clunky nailed boots, and men and women of almost every nationality and race, all dressed in the latest fashions of their respective countries, intermingled in the short length of the dusty main street.

Banff, like the mountains that gave it birth, was midway between the era of

earliest exploration and the age of mass commercialism. The David Thompsons and the Reverend Robert Rundles had come and gone, but the multitudes of highly mobile middle-class sightseers racing through the mountains at ever-increasing speed and in ever-increasing numbers had yet to arrive.

The Canadian Rockies in 1903 offered a playground for the not-so-idle rich and for climbers from England and the continent seeking first ascents comparable to those that had been exhausted in the Alps a decade earlier. They found new tracts of wilderness that had been charted and measured only in the most cursory manner by cartographers and scientists. Those who were somehow afflicted found the promise of health in the mineral hot springs, which were guaranteed to be "especially

efficacious for the cure of rheumatic, gouty and allied conditions." For a young photographer the Rockies offered a time and place of high excitement, wild-west romantic notions, and soaring mountains and shifting light to stir both spirit and eye. It was the beginning of a 40-year affair.

Byron Hill Harmon, born on February 9, 1876, near Tacoma, Washington, was one of three children of Hili and Clara Smith Harmon. The parents were of pioneer stock, Clara's family journeying from Indiana to Washington in 1851 via the Oregon Trail, Hill's family following a more circuitous route to the West from New Brunswick and New York.

Clara exhibited all the characteristics expected of a child raised on a donation claim (let alone the second white person born on one of the islands of Puget Sound): resourcefulness and self-reliance, a respect for nature, and a compassion for others. She needed all of those qualities, for her husband disappeared shortly after Byron's birth and she was left with the sole responsibility for her three children. Working as a matron on one of the Puget Sound reservations, she kept her family together and exposed her children to the Native character and native skills, an experience that would stand Byron in good stead in later years in the Rockies.

As a young boy Harmon had serious illnesses, suffering through typhoid on two occasions and struggling constantly against asthma. This affliction greatly influenced his decision to settle in the Rockies, where the clear, dry air granted him almost complete relief. The asthma stayed with him all his life, however, and occasionally when he returned to a coastal climate he suffered relapses so severe that he was forced to sleep sitting up in a chair to keep his lungs clear.

In his teens he exhibited two traits that would persist throughout his life: a predilection for working with his hands, creating and building objects of his own design, and a penchant for photography. Kodak marketed the first roll film in the late 1880s, and the company, using the slogan "You push the button, we do the rest," went to great lengths to convince the American public that photography was no longer a science restricted to a professionally trained elite. Being unable to afford one of the advertised cameras, Harmon brought his talents to bear on a wooden

box and fashioned a crude product of his own – a lensless pinhole affair that gave him his first images. Whatever the results of that early camera, they obviously encouraged him to continue with photography. In fact he turned to it for a living, after a short stint working in a mill not only proved uncreative but also aggravated his asthma.

He opened a small portrait studio in Tacoma, probably in the mid-1890s, and the story of his humble beginnings as a professional photographer became a favourite one in his later, more comfortable years.

Once the young photographer had rented a building and equipped it with the necessary paraphernalia for developing and printing portraits, he was totally out of cash and well beyond his line of credit. Embarrassingly, he was a photographer without film for his cameras. Unperturbed, he welcomed his first client and calmly took a photograph sans film, receiving payment in advance. When the client returned the next day to collect the portrait, Harmon announced that he was not pleased with the results and that the process would have to be repeated. Another portrait was taken, this time with film purchased with the down payment, and Harmon was in business. Whether or not his ploy was a product of desperation or a premeditated risk or both, it exemplifies the ingenuity and confidence Harmon exhibited again and again in his photographic career.

Some time toward the end of the 1890s, Harmon decided his asthma and his photography both needed a change of scenery.

Reducing his studio to that which he could pack into two or three valises, he closed shop and left town – an itinerant photographer off to see the world. For two or three years he travelled throughout the American Southwest and on to the eastern seaboard, to New York, and thence back west across Canada. His work was typical of the photography done in those days: stiff, formal Victorian portraits of couples and families, and slightly less formal poses of tradesmen standing, arms crossed, in front of the apparatus of their trade. It was not a lucrative way to make a living, but his presence would invariably arouse the collective curiosity of the small American and Canadian towns through which he travelled.

If Harmon's first visit to Banff was a short one, it was an important one. While soaking in the hot springs one day, he struck up a conversation with a local who informed him that despite the possibilities for a photographer in a town like Banff, there was as yet no permanent studio. Harmon was quick to recognize the potential for asthmatic relief in the high mountain air, and there is little doubt that the mountains themselves struck a highly responsive chord in him, for within a year he was back in what he termed "that part of Canada which stands on end." He embarked on his life's work: photographing every major peak and glacier in the Rocky and Selkirk mountains in as many different moods and seasons as possible. It was a task that would end only when he could no longer travel deep into the mountain wilderness – within the deep glacier-scoured valleys; over miles of limestone and quartzite ridges and peaks; across acres of tumbling, fissured glacial ice and the fast-flowing silted rivers; and among the peculiarly turquoise-tinted lakes that might reflect 20 shades of light at any one moment.

Before returning to Banff to live, however, Harmon had some odds and ends to look after in the foothills, and he returned for a short while to High River, where he had been working before his mountain visit. There he exhibited a typical "seize-the-moment" impulsiveness by photographing a much-wanted gunman who had fled the US and was creating no small concern in the towns along the eastern slopes of the Rockies. Hiding behind a stout brick chimney on a main-street roof, Harmon was able to photograph him undetected. The resulting print, of a wild-west desperado with a revolver on his hip, captured the imagination of the East and was carried by many of the major papers. It brought Harmon his first national recognition.

The combination of a healthy climate, magnificent scenery, and a chance to make a decent living must have had great appeal for Harmon. A long-time resident recalls the photographer as poor and in ill-health when he returned to Banff. He was seen about town in a white shirt, overalls, a large straw "sou'wester" hat, typical of those found in the American Southwest at the time, and short boots with no socks – a stocky man of medium height in peculiar clothes practising a peculiar trade.

Although he continued his portraiture in his first months in Banff, Harmon's photographic emphasis quickly shifted to the town's mountain setting and he began producing a line of "mountain views" to sell to the tourists the Canadian Pacific brought to town. By 1907 he had accumulated enough views to advertise the largest collection of Canadian Rockies postcards in existence ("over 100 assorted views"), and he had saved enough money to pack away his valises and move into a tiny building on Banff Avenue that he converted into an effective working area by knocking a couple of skylights into the low shed roof.

From that time on, Harmon rarely took a formal indoor portrait. Only a few photographs of Stoney Natives, taken over the years at the annual Banff Indian Days, present full-frame, close-up visualizations of character; he was more interested in man in a larger context. Faces are frequently a part of his mountain photographs, but they almost inevitably appear as foils in an environmental drama. Harmon's preference was for landscape. "I'd rather shoot mountains than people," he would say, "because mountains, at least, stand still."

With his health much improved, he began to pursue the alpine pastimes of the day – hiking, riding, and climbing but always carrying the heavy, awkward photographic equipment of the early 1900s: 4" x 5" and 5" x 7" view cameras (and, after 1910, a movie camera), wooden tripods, changing bag, extra film packs, and glass plates.

At the turn of the century Banff was a centre for mountain climbing, perhaps even more than it is today, because of the large number of unnamed and unclimbed peaks in the immediate vicinity. As a Victorian sport, climbing had no equal, and with all the great peaks of Europe conquered by the 1880s, alpinists turned their alpenstocks toward the unexplored regions of Canada. The CPR, not missing a trick, imported European climbing guides to escort tourists and alpinists to the summits of the Rockies and Selkirks, and such international figures as Edward Whymper of the Matterhorn became familiar faces in the Banff environs.

With so much activity in the area, it was only a matter of time before the sport became formally organized, and in March 1906 the Alpine Club of Canada (ACC) was founded. After three years in the mountains, Harmon had become such an ardent alpinist and Rockies booster that he became a charter member of the Club and its official photographer. He was eager to use his skills to fulfil the dictates of the Club 's charter, which called for "the cultivation of art in relation to mountain scenery" and "the exploration and study of Canada's alpine tracts; and, with that in mind ... [the gathering of] literary material and photographs for publication.'

The major event of the ACC's year was its climbing camp, held each year at a different spot in either the Rockies or Selkirks, featuring a week of exploring, hiking, and climbing. For most members it meant a moderately priced vacation in the mountains (all extended travel at that time was by pack train, an expensive proposition). For Harmon it meant a priceless opportunity to expand both his photographic and alpine experiences, and he rarely missed a summer camp during his early years of ACC involvement.

Harmon's work with the ACC was critically important to his career, because it opened up not only new territory for him but also important channels for recognition of his work. The *Canadian Alpine Journal*, distributed to members across North America and abroad, featured many of his photographs and, given the curiosity about the Rockies at the time, brought his images to the attention of alpinists, explorers, scientists, and editors throughout the world. And certainly the early ACC trips provided the basis for much of his collection, which today is made up of some 6500 negatives and plates.

Club activities brought Harmon into close contact with the most colourful men in the Rockies, men who exerted great influence on his life. There were the European guides such as Conrad Kain, Edward Feuz, and Rudolf Aemmer, men famous for their strength and daring who, collectively, never lost a single client. There were the packers and outfitters like Jimmy Simpson, Bill Peyto, and the Brewster brothers, horsemen whose ability to turn an invective phrase against an "ornery cayuse" never failed to astound the dudes and was matched only by their ability to bend the wilderness to meet their own ends. And there were the explorers, scientists, and surveyors like Charles Walcott, secretary of the Smithsonian Institution, and A.O. Wheeler, founder, director, and

first president of the ACC and one of Canada's foremost surveyors and cartographers. From such men Harmon learned the secrets of mountain life, from the subtleties of the alpinists' knots and the packers' diamond hitch to the trick of drying wet matches in his hair. With them he formed his closest friendships – alliances that lasted long after his most active days on the trail.

His role as ACC photographer gave Harmon a unique position in its hierarchy, and on several occasions he was asked to accompany special expeditions sponsored by the Club or its leaders. These trips had immeasurable importance for him, giving him a chance at extended travel in areas he probably wouldn't have seen by himself. Two journeys deserve particular mention.

In the fall of 1910, A.O. Wheeler asked Harmon to accompany a three-week trip into the Purcell Range, west of the Rockies and south of the Selkirks. The expedition had two purposes: to explore and map an area new to Wheeler, and to give a visiting Himalayan mountaineer and arctic explorer, Dr. T.G. Longstaff, a chance to hunt in the wilds of western Canada. In his memoirs, Longstaff remembers the mountains in 1910 as being at once beautiful and threatening:

There is nothing more beautiful in any other mountain scene, but its menace is inescapable. The secret may lie in the density of the forests and their pathlessness: here is no reassurance of ancient tracks, no passes crossed by generations of caravans. The mountains of Europe and

Asia recall gods and dryads and the long procession of man. These empty wilds are peopled only by our bare imagination, apt to primitive terror: there is no past except starvation.[1]

One man's menace, however, is another man's lure, and to all but the packers (who eventually had to turn back because they couldn't get the horses through the dense forests of the Purcells) the trip was an exciting and successful tour. Wheeler managed his survey; Longstaff was so successful in his hunting that modern conservationists cringe when reading how he took three grizzlies in one afternoon (an event that Harmon photographed and turned into a best-selling postcard); and Harmon got his photographs.

Just as the alpinists of the day were pleased to capture a new peak by hand and rope, so Harmon was pleased to capture a new area on film, and the Purcells offered a particularly rewarding prize. Early in the trip, Harmon spent a day with the packers ahead of the main party clearing a trail for the horses. when he returned to camp that evening he was in an exultant mood. He had, he reported, discovered a massive glacier, the ice of which was pierced by what Longstaff later described as "a collection of the most striking *aiguilles* I ever saw in the western mountains ... [which] shot up from behind the glacier like arctic nunataks out of an icecap: quite sheer, without a speck of snow" [p. 231]. The glacier, first known as Harmon's Glacier, is today called the Bugaboo Glacier and its expanse of ice and the surrounding peaks constitute one of North America's most famous climbing and skiing areas.

Descriptions of the trip written by both Longstaff and Conrad Kain, the party's alpine guide, provide the beginnings of a portrait of Harmon as a trail companion. Longstaff recalls him as "a very good goer" and states that "a hardier companion none could wish for." Harmon was, as usual, "inseparable from his beloved camera," and was indefatigable in his efforts to catch the images he wanted. A man of nearly boundless energy, he was more than willing to help the packers cut trail or to help rope up the horses "as if they were tourists" and yard them up a particularly steep section of trail. On one occasion he hiked a continuous 36 mountain miles with full pack and camera gear, a feat few men would attempt, let alone complete!

He also possessed a keen, interested mind and a quirky sense of humor, traits that endeared him to those with whom he travelled. Though he is remembered as a quiet, private person, genial but slightly aloof, he was never above participating in the fireside activities so important to trail life. Both Harmon and Kain were mirthful souls at the fireside, and the two of them together had a special ability to keep a camp in high spirits. Kain, in *Where the Clouds Can Go*, remembered the following scene after a particularly rough day on the Purcells trip:

To improve our humour we held an Indian dance. Dr. Longstaff and the two packers put on bear hides and I the goat skin. Mr. Harmon, the photographer, was the band.

His instrument the pans. So we danced about the fire, making a terrific din.[2]

The following summer Harmon again took to the trail with Wheeler and Kain in a larger party, including four scientists from the prestigious Smithsonian Institution, on a three-month trip to the Rainbow Mountains in what are now Jasper National Park and Mt. Robson Provincial Park. The purpose of the expedition was threefold: Wheeler wanted to survey the region and investigate the Mt. Robson environs as a possible site for a future ACC camp, and the Smithsonian men were interested in the flora, fauna, and geology of the area.[3]

It was a major trip into an uncharted region and, as might be expected, did not lack excitement. Kain described some of the problems in his diary, not the least of which was travelling with a photographer:

Not incorrectly is this called the "Wild West." No houses, no roads; only old Indian trails. The valleys are wet and boggy, and one often sinks in to the knees. We have already ascended some mountains, but the getting there! On our first excursion we were almost buried by an avalanche, and Mr. Harmon had to photograph it at the very worst moment![4]

This trip, Harmon's most extended mountain tour, was important, matched only by a trip to the Columbia Icefield thirteen years later. After 90 days in the wilderness even a mediocre photographer restricted to the valley bottoms could be expected to bring in a few decent plates. For an avid

and seasoned photographer, on an expedition that scaled more than 30 peaks, there was bound to be an abundant harvest. And, judging from the results, Harmon was able to add credibility to his dictum that in order to know and photograph the mountains one had to walk through them, shooting them from the valleys up and from the summits down. Many of the finest prints in the collection date from this 1911 trip. Viewed collectively, they are a superb document of mountain travel and exploration. If one cares to look farther, reading between the highlights and the shadows, one finds a special understanding of the mountains and what it means to measure one's life against them. The underlying exuberance of exploration, the dare and labor and ecstasy of the ascent, the challenge of the hunt, and the quiet days in camp are all there; but above all is the heady feeling of being *here*, in a vast and nameless place, close to the extreme leading edge of life. Harmon was not an articulate philosopher, but these photographs of the broad rock faces and undulating glaciers, of men dwarfed on immense icefields, of climbers working on rock, snow, and ice, or weary but self-satisfied explorers resting in camp, speak eloquently for him.

Aside from the photographic aspects of the trip, two events occurred that were a source of great personal pride to Harmon. He and Kain achieved the first ascent of Mt. Resplendent, at 3362 metres a major peak in the Mt. Robson area, and he was in the first party to cross through the mountains "from steel to steel," from the Grand Trunk Pacific Railway at Fitzhugh (now Jasper) to the Canadian Pacific Railway at Laggan (now Lake Louise).

The ascent of Mt. Resplendent was particularly gratifying, although the two men had to use a certain amount of dissimulation to make the climb. At the trip's outset, Wheeler had promised Harmon, Kain, and another well-known climber, the Reverend G.B. Kinney, a chance at the unclimbed Mt. Robson, the highest peak in the Canadian Rockies (3891 metres), if they would accompany the expedition. When the group reached the Robson area, however, Wheeler began to find excuses for keeping the men away from the big peaks. The trio became convinced that Wheeler wanted to save the major first ascents for a later ACC camp, and so it was that minor insurrections sprang up in camp. Harmon and Kain left camp one morning on the pretext of making a glacier reconnaissance in the great Robson amphitheatre and came back late with the ascent of Mt. Resplendent secured. Kain added further fire to Wheeler's ill-suppressed fury when, a few days later, under the pretense of walking down the Emperor Falls gorge, he undertook a solo overnight climb of Mt. Whitehorn, a climb he later described as "one of the craziest and most foolhardy undertakings that I ever made in the mountains."[5] Yet his rationale was easily understood by his alpinist companions: " I could stand it no longer," he wrote, "being among beautiful mountains without climbing one."

The return to Banff had its points of interest as well. Leaving Maligne Lake (now part of Jasper National Park) on September 18, a late start, the party encountered heavy snowfall in the high mountain passes close to the Continental Divide. Harmon found the logistics of moving a pack train through deep snow so photographically stimulating that years later, on his journey to the Columbia Icefield, he deliberately set out to duplicate the experience!

Trips such as the Purcell and Rainbow expeditions were exceptional opportunities and a far cry from the usual ACC climbing-camp endeavors, which Harmon enjoyed but ultimately found restrictive to his art. Travelling with large groups of people, keeping their pace (literally roped to their pace on the climbs), and going where they went often prevented him from catching the images he sought. His style required both a freedom to roam and a freedom to wait. An auspicious meeting of light and subject was not an event that occurred on demand, and on occasion Harmon's photographic "lingerings" would become major feats of endurance.[6] Thus as years passed the photographer began to organize his own trips, making it clear to everyone at the outset that it was a photographic expedition to be taken at a photographer's pace. It should be noted, though, that Harmon remained a strong supporter of any group effort that would involve people with the mountains. He maintained close contacts with the ACC and was a founding member of both the Trail Riders of the Canadian Rockies, established in 1924, and the Sky Line Trail Hikers of the Canadian Rockies, organized in 1933.

Recognition came early. By 1908 the Banff paper, the *Crag and Canyon*, was keeping a close eye on the activities of the "artistic photographer," and in 1910, Longstaff, in an article on the Purcells trip in the *Canadian Alpine Journal* opined that the expedition was "fortunate in getting Mr. Byron Harmon ... whose Canadian mountain photographs are so deservedly popular, to come with us ..." His pictures of both trail life and activities in and around Banff were being picked up by the national news services and his widening circle of influential trail companions carried word of his work back home with them.

Harmon also gained stature through an impressive line of postcards,[7] viewbooks, and calenders that were mass produced by companies in Germany, England, and Vancouver at first, and later in his own Banff studio. Sales centred on the CPR, the only means of transportation through the Rockies in those days, and the railroad "newsies" would peddle his works in the trains from Winnipeg to Vancouver. Catering to this market, Harmon produced viewbooks and cards collectively entitled "Along the Line of the CPR," and included a railroad motif in many of the photographs.

In his personal and business life, Harmon maintained the same level of energy, ingenuity, and perseverance that he displayed on the trail. In 1908 he purchased an old livery barn across the street from his original location and converted it into a new and expanded darkroom and curio shop, and in 1912 he bought an adjoining lot on which he built a moving-picture theatre that featured not only "fresh films daily," but variety nights and, during

World War I, various patriotic fund raisers. Unfortunately the theatre burned to the ground in January 1917. The fire cost Harmon an estimated thirteen thousand dollars and destroyed not only the theatre but portions of his working area next door, which meant a partial loss of his collection of stills and movie footage and most of his stock on hand. It was totally typical of the man, though, that within two or three days he had farmed out various phases of his business to different places in town and was back at work, plotting new schemes for his burned-out building.

Indeed, Harmon proved to be the archetypal free-enterprise entrepreneur. Seldom a year went by without some major renovation in the "Harmon Block," and over the years his buildings included various combinations of the studio, a theatre, a curio shop, a drug store, a fountain lunch and tea shop, a book store and lending library, a woollen shop, and even a beauty parlor, many of them occupying a common area. His passion for designing and building fit in perfectly with the boom in technological gadgetry prior to World War I, and he was forever trying out new ideas. His shops featured the first gas lights in Banff, the first ice cream maker, the first neon sign, probably the first radio and phonograph, one of the first postcard machines in western Canada (capable of producing 4000 cards a day), and God only knows what else. He designed and built much of the equipment used in his darkroom, built the screen used in the theatre, and devised an ingenious ventilating system for the theatre, incorporating hollow beams that ran the length of the building. He was always amused to find that someone in town had "borrowed" one of his business innovations for their own shop, and he would invariably smile and say, "That's all right. There are plenty more ideas where that one came from."

He was also somewhat of a speculator and at various times had amounts of money invested in drilling and mining operations. Receiving word that one such investment was not perhaps entirely above moral (and perhaps legal) reproach, he quickly pulled his shares and walked away with a good profit – in early 1929.

Making films was yet another vocation that Harmon pursued. Although nearly all of his footage has disappeared over the years, movies were important to him for both pleasure and profit. From the early teens on he devoted more and more time to film technique and technology, and some of his later journeys were specifically referred to as movie trips. A fair portion of his footage was purchased by Fox Movietone News for national and international distribution

Harmon's photographic ability and entrepreneurial inventiveness were matched by a strong sense of civic responsibility. Remembered by all as a "model citizen," he was a founding member of the Banff Board of Trade (a forerunner of both the Chamber of Commerce and the Banff Advisory Council), a member of the school board for many years, an organizer of the Banff Conservative Association, a charter member of the Rotary Club, a major investor in a newspaper meant to compete with the *Crag and Canyon* – making him an unwilling participant in an ensuing political feud, and a member of numerous other local committees, boards, and associations. For its part, the town was more than pleased with its photographer, who was keeping Banff well in the eye of the North American press. As the *Crag* put it in 1919:

Byron Harmon is the best asset Banff has in the line of advertising the village to the outside world. Nothing of importance occurs but he is present with his movie camera, and the Harmon films of Banff and the mountains are becoming known wherever there is a movie house.

In the same year he received the culminating recognition of his career. The Government of Canada, with the Alpine Club of Canada, asked Harmon to be one of four representatives to the International Congress of Alpinism in Monaco in May 1920. The trip was a triumph. His old trail companion, Wheeler, reported in the *Canadian Alpine Journal* (1920):

With the whole-hearted assistance of Mr. Harmon your director was enabled to arrange a magnificent exhibit of photographic enlargements, some 150 in number, of the most striking scenic features of the Canadian Rocky Mountains, comprised chiefly of Mr. Harmon's beautiful pictures and unsurpassed motion films ...

The exhibition was, by all reviews, a showstopper, particularly the movies. According to Wheeler, "they carried his audience off its feet and [Harmon] was called on to show them again and again throughout the duration of the Congress."

Monaco, as it turned out, was but one of several locations in which the exhibit received rave reviews. On his way there Harmon had exhibited his prints on the floor of the Canadian House of Commons (selling prints to nearly all the members of Parliament), and after the Congress he showed his films before the Royal Geographical Society in London and the Royal Scottish Geographical Society in Glasgow, Aberdeen, and Edinburgh.

On the strength of the 1920 jaunt, Harmon returned to Europe in the winter of 1923–4, exhibiting prints and showing films in the major centres of France, Germany, and Great Britain and returning with contracts for over 15,000 feet of film no small amount in the early twenties. The mountain photographer had arrived.

Despite his successes, Harmon remained a quiet and modest person, the sort of man, according to oldtimers, whom one might take for granted. An immaculate dresser in town, a near teetotaller and nonsmoker, he avoided the social activities of Banff, preferring to spend his time with his family[8] or his work. Not that he was unfriendly; he merely had other things on his mind than curling, cards, and dancing, the three major Banff social pastimes.

One of the things on his mind, of course, was his continuing work with the Rockies and the Selkirks. Harmon told Lewis Freeman, a freelance writer and adventurer, of his master plan in the late summer of 1920 when the two men met at the Lake of the Hanging Glaciers. He had allotted himself twenty years to photograph every major peak and glacier in the Rockies and Selkirks and, having finished the first run-through, would be ready to start all over again. At their first meeting Harmon was sitting out a seemingly interminable period of bad weather – waiting, as he so often did, for the light. Freeman took note of the wait and later wrote:

It was in that quiet, patient, persistent way that he had been photographing the mountains of the Canadian West for many years, and it will be just in that way he will continue until he shall have attained somewhere near to the high goal he has set for his lifework ... It is a privilege to have met an artist who works with so fine a spirit, who has set himself so high an ideal.[9]

Whereas the early exploring sessions with Wheeler had been exciting, Harmon's later photographic and movie trips were adventurous to the point of danger. He was forever ready to set up a shot to capture the most romantic implication of any given event. If there existed a choice between doing something an easy way or doing it in an arduous but more visually exciting way, Harmon would invariably opt for excitement.

Nor was he against accelerating the course of nature occasionally to suit his purposes. In 1922 he joined forces with his old friend Conrad Kain and two clients from Minneapolis on a pack-train trip to the Lake of the Hanging Glaciers to film a massive avalanche. He had confidence that just such an occurrence might happen while he was at the lake, since he and Kain had secreted 36 sticks of dynamite into the pack duffel. Cora Best, one of the Minneapolis dudes, graphically described the resulting high comedy for the *Canadian Alpine Journal* (1923):

Conrad went over and dug a hole in the ice and placed his dynamite, tamped it down and lighted the fuse. When he came back he remarked that something should come loose as there were seventeen sticks about to let go. Harmon took a last anxious look into the finder ... He mopped his face and looked along the line to see if everything was ready. It was ...The earth shook, the air turned purple: Mother Nature agonized, and a few pounds of ice tinkled off into the water as the smoke drifted away. But, of course, that was understood. We were waiting for the aftermath, the mighty avalanche we were sure to get.

Now, when Old Bill [a pack horse] had been unloaded he had strolled off to browse on some tufts of green and no one had given him a second thought. When the first report of the discharge took place, Old Bill started a little charge of his own ... He came down the stretch hitting on all fours, his mane flying, his nostrils dilated and flaming, his eyes holding the fire of battle. He hit Harmon first! Down went the camera and Old Bill walked up the spine of the vanquished photographer, hit the second, third and fourth cameras with sickening precision and careered off down the valley. And then it happened! The whole top of the mountain eased off a bit, toppled and crashed to the glacier below in the mightiest of mighty avalanches.

Harmon organized his last extended trip into the mountains in 1924 – a 70-day, 500-mile trip to Jasper via the Columbia Icefield and the headwaters of the Athabasca River – hoping to photograph the last remaining obstacles to the completion of his work: the mountains and glaciers of the Columbia Group. With two or three major deviations, the route followed the line of the Icefields Parkway that runs today from Lake Louise to Jasper.

Of all his trips, it is the best documented, for accompanying Harmon was Lewis Freeman, who wrote an unfortunately exaggerated account of the expedition for the *National Geographic* (using many of Harmon's photographs – and later wrote *On the Roof of the Rockies,* about the trials and tribulations of the trip. The book is dedicated "To Byron Harmon, who, through his photographs, has given the Canadian Rockies to the World."

Harmon's propensity for the exciting shot led them into some rather peculiar situations. Forgoing the obvious and easy river fords, Harmon would repeatedly ask the packers to drive the horses through some slightly rougher waters, in one case driving a good portion of the pack train into, around, and under a log jam. On another occasion, failing to get the desired footage of a mountain goat's being shot and falling off a high precipice, Harmon had his companions rig up a goat carcass so it would "leap" off a cliff while being filmed from below. The goat leapt, all

right, and came within millimetres of driving Byron a good distance into the glacial ice he was shooting from.

The pack train was also outfitted with a radio and passenger pigeons,[10] Freeman wishing to prove that radio reception was possible in the wilds of the western mountains, and Harmon wanting to see if the pigeons could thread their way through the peaks back to Banff. The radio worked extremely well, both as a receiving instrument and as a prop for an endless array of photographs, but the pigeons were a major disappointment.

One other experiment consisted of crossing a glacier tongue with the pack horses. This improbable action was taken both to give the party a better look at the mother icefield, the Columbia, and to avoid travelling an alternate route consisting of 40 miles of flooded river flats. Although some problems were encountered in getting the horses off the glacier, where they had to slide down a narrow ramp of ice flanked by deep crevasses, the traverse went smoothly and Harmon put the event to good photographic use.

Despite the adventures, or misadventures, of the journey, the expedition was successful, right down to the calculated snow storm in Jonas Pass on the way home, and Harmon returned with 400 stills and some 7000 feet of film. It was somehow fitting that he had been forced to wait eight days for the light to reach Mt. Columbia, the second highest peak in the Rockies, the monarch of the Icefield and one of the last mountains he felt he needed in his collection. It wasn't until the after-

noon of the eighth day, after time, food, and patience were exhausted and the pack train had been sent on down the valley, that Harmon, lingering behind, caught his image. The light played on the summit for less than 40 minutes. At the end of those minutes, Freeman recalled, "The black rectangles of paper torn from Harmon's film packs were piled up behind his tripods like the brass shells around a hard-pumped machine gun at the end of a battle."

Harmon did not abandon the mountains after his 1924 Icefield trip. Winter and summer he was out with dog team and pack horse, with skier and hiker, but the Icefield expedition was his last extensive exploratory journey. He found that his business required more and more time, as did his desire to see new places and experience new things. Nearly every year from the mid-20s on he managed a major trip outside the mountains, often travelling to the American Southwest, but often as not to more remote, exotic spots: Mexico, Guatemala, Hong Kong, Europe, and once, in 1930, around the world. No matter where he went, he always insisted upon his return that the Rockies were the best of all and, indeed, wherever he went he carried photographs and films to show all who might be interested.[11]

His last years in Banff were relatively quiet ones. High blood pressure and diminishing sight and hearing troubled him increasingly, but he remained a keen and interested observer of things around him. His love of the mountains and its inhabitants burned as brightly as ever, as did his own particular sense of humour. His son

Don one day reproached him for swatting at flies that were on the outside of a screen door and Harmon retorted, smiling, "Well, this way, you see, I stun their legs. Then they fall to the sidewalk and break their necks."

During the spring of 1942 his health took a turn for the worse and he was admitted to the hospital several times for high blood pressure. It was not easy for a man with such vitality and so much interest in life to accept the inevitable slowing down, and he lamented to a visiting friend one day that there seemed to be no compensation for good living.

His death on July 10, 1942, at the age of sixty-six, was sadly noted by his old acquaintance A.O. Wheeler in the *Canadian Alpine Journal* (1943): "In the art and science of photography," he wrote, "he was outstanding *par excellence* ... We liked him well and shall not readily forget him and the living record of his life work."

NOTES

1. Tom Longstaff, *This My Voyage* (London: John Murray, 1950), p. 218

2. Conrad Kain, *Where the Clouds Can Go.* (New York: The American Alpine Club, 1935), p. 273. (Published posthumously. Edited, with additional chapters, by J. Monroe Thorington)

3. It has been suggested that, once the fur trade was finished and the railway run through, there was only one reason for expeditions in the Rockies: to have a good time. The rest was rationale.

4. Kain, *Where the Clouds Can Go*, p. 282.

5. *Canadian Alpine Journal*, 6 (1914)

6. Walter Wilcox, in *The Canadian Rockies* (New York: G.P. Putnam's Sons, 1913), writes eloquently of the need for patience if one is to photograph the Rockies successfully: "... it is easy to prove that in an entire year there are only a few minutes, or at the most, a few hours in which the conditions are perfect for exposing a plate. Let us say that only during three months is the ground free of snow. Of these ninety days the large majority will be either stormy, or overcast, or very windy, and of the remainder some will be densely smoky, or too brilliant, so that the problem quickly narrows down to a possible 10 perfect days. In each of these there will be only one or two hours in which the direction of sunlight is favourable for any given picture, and during these hours only a short time in which the ever-drifting clouds are properly grouped, the water surface unruffled, and the sunlight falling on foreground, or distance, or wherever you desire it to be."(p. 213)

7. The status of the postcard was considerably greater in the early 1900s than it is today. Between 1880 and the Great War the postcard had great appeal; and, in fact, a special word, "delitilology," was coined to denote the study of postcards. Most of the early cards were printed in Germany, where the best lithography was done.

8. His first marriage was to Maud Moore in either 1909 or 1910. Three children – Aileen, Lloyd, and Don – were born in 1912, 1914, and 1917. Don was born on the same night the theatre burned down, something Harmon used to tease him about: "Worst time of my life," he would say, "two disasters in one night." A second marriage, to Rebecca Pearl Shearer, took place in Seattle in 1928.

9. Lewis Freeman, *On the Roof of the Rockies* (New York: Dodd, Mead and Co., 1925), p. 11

10. Harmon was an avid naturalist and was sympathetic to all forms of animal life – so much so, in fact, that he never owned a rifle and would hunt only when absolutely necessary. Throughout his life he kept various pets, including dogs, pigeons, and a squirrel that used to ride in his coat pocket. At one point he brought home a porcupine for his children, and deer were always encouraged to wander into his house from the street to eat food scraps in the pantry.

11. A promoter to the end, Byron once left for the Southwest with his car "specially arranged for the tour with the best and latest view of Lake Louise filling the right hand window ... a panoramic view of the Bow River filling the back window, and a picture of Mount Columbia in the left window ..." (*Crag and Canyon*, 1938)

NOTE ABOUT THE PHOTOGRAPHIC CAPTIONS:

Persons and features in the photographic captions are mentioned from left to right.

JOE STEVENS

THE CAVE AND BASIN BATHHOUSE CA 1910

The discovery of sulphur springs on Sulphur Mountain in 1883 by three railroad construction workers, William and Tom McCardell and Frank McCabe, triggered a furor. It led to the establishment of Banff Hot Springs Reserve by the federal government in 1885. In June 1887 the name was changed to Rocky Mountains Park and the area was expanded to the foothills beyond Devils Gap, considerably beyond the present eastern boundary of Banff National Park. In 1907 the park was expanded again to include Lake Louise, an area of 3000 square miles.

TOM WILSON ON BANFF AVENUE, CA 1905

Tom Wilson, guide, outfitter and local legend, originally came to Banff with Major Roberts who surveyed the route for the Canadian Pacific Railway through the Canadian Rockies and adjacent Selkirk Mountains in the 1880s.

THE CAVE AND BASIN BATHHOUSE CA 1910

Site of the original discovery of hot springs in Banff, The Cave and Basin was an instant hit with visitors and has seen many changes and expansions through the years. It is now a major interpretive centre for Canada's national parks.

MRS. GRIFFITH AT THE ACC CAMP IN YOHO VALLEY, 1906

The Alpine Club of Canada (ACC) was formed in 1906 and held its first mountaineering camp that summer at Laughing Falls in Yoho Valley. Mountaineers and prospective mountaineers came from all over Canada, US, and Great Britain.

THE FIRST ACC CAMP AT LAUGHING FALLS, 1906

Founding member Byron Harmon graduated to active membership by climbing Mt. Vice President at this camp. He was official photographer of the club for many years to come.

THREE LADIES AT AN EARLY ACC CAMP

Unlike the English and American alpine clubs, women were welcome members of the Alpine Club of Canada. One of the driving forces in founding the ACC was Elizabeth Parker of Winnipeg.

CONRAD KAIN, "GUIDE IN THE NEW WORLD," 1909

Conrad Kain was an experienced guide from Austria who came to Canada in 1909 to work for the Alpine Club of Canada. He eventually settled in the Selkirks and was probably the most illustrious guide in Canadian Rockies mountain-eering history.

AT THE GIANT STEPS IN PARADISE VALLEY, 1907

The second (annual) ACC camp was held in Paradise Valley, a beautiful valley between Lake Louise and Moraine Lake. One of the unusual features of this valley is a spectacular series of cascades and waterfalls beneath the slopes of Mt. Hungabee called the Giant Steps.

A GROUP OF CLIMBERS IN PARADISE VALLEY, 1907
Climbing gear at these early ACC camps included hob-nailed, knee-high leather boots and alpenstocks, the long walking staffs with metal tips. Women still wore skirts or voluminous knee-length britches.

ASCENDING A SNOW SLOPE

The perfectly posed shot is a hallmark that appears repeatedly in Byron Harmon's photography. In these early days of mountaineering, photography was still a marvel and a novelty, and people were eager to co-operate.

DESCENDING A SNOW SLOPE

This is another posed shot. Snow slopes provide glorious opportunities for glissading, usually on one's feet but occasionally in more ignominious positions.

INTERIOR OF THE RESTHOUSE ON SADDLEBACK

The CPR built lodges and small teahouses around the Lake Louise area early this century. The resthouse on Saddleback is gone now, but the teahouses at Lake Agnes and Plain of Six Glaciers and lodges at Lake O'Hara, Skoki, and Twin Falls still operate.

AT THE CONSOLATION VALLEY ACC CAMP, 1910

Humor was always a strong characteristic of Byron Harmon. He loved to point up the adventure and excitement of these early camps with set-up photographs that illustrated camp life, as well as pulling the leg of the serious mountaineer.

AT THE
CONSOLATION
VALLEY ACC
CAMP,
1910
The same group of
climbers as in the
previous photo
pose for this
photograph in
their nightshirts.
The camp was
attended by
climbers from the
alpine clubs of
England, US,
Germany-Austria,
Italy, and Switzer-
land.

MT. HUNGABEE
FROM MT.
VICTORIA

CLIMBER
LOOKING DOWN
THE ROBSON
GLACIER

ASCENDING MT. HUBER, 1909

The 1909 ACC camp was held at Lake O'Hara, a beautiful, isolated valley in Yoho National Park. It is separated from Lake Louise Valley by Mt. Victoria and Mt. Lefroy. In this photograph, a group of climbers ascends the arête on Mt. Huber.

ASCENDING MT. HUBER, 1909

A great deal of planning goes into a photograph such as this. The photographer has to position himself correctly and anticipate the right time to capture the line of climbers traversing the snow slope.

AN AVALANCHE IN THE SELKIRKS, 1910

On March 5, 1910 a colossal avalanche buried Snow Shed #14 on the Canadian Pacific line in the Selkirk Range west of the Rockies, killing 62 men. Bodies were dug out with shovels.

CLEARING A PATH THROUGH THE AVALANCHE, 1910

A snow shovel was fitted to the front of the locomotive to clear a path through the avalanche along the railway line.

AVALANCHE IN THE SELKIRKS, 1910

Both the Canadian Pacific Railway and the Trans-Canada Highway pass through steep valleys in the Selkirk Range where the snowfall is heavy and the danger from avalanches great. Snowsheds cover vulnerable areas of both the railway line and the highway, but it is still possible to be trapped inside a snowshed or caught by an avalanche in an unprotected area.

AN ACC GROUP
ASCENDING A
SNOW SLOPE

MT. CARNARVON FROM EMERALD PASS AREA, 1910

The climbers in this photograph are Thomas Longstaff, Fred Bell, Henry Worstold, and E.O. Wheeler. Dr. T.G. Longstaff, a physiologist from England, was noted for his climbs and explorations in the Himalayas and the Arctic. He spent the summer of 1910 in Canada. Members of the ACC escorted him and other visitors to the Yoho Valley region following the annual camp in Consolation Valley.

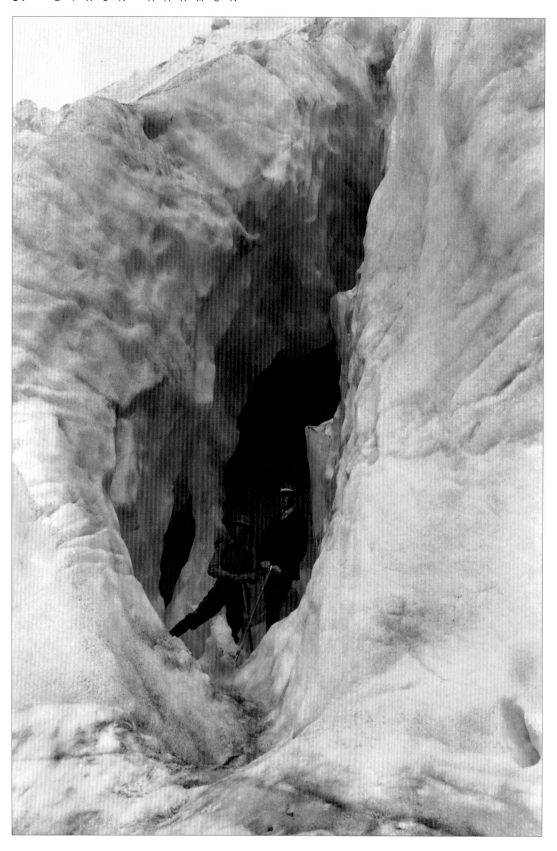

A CREVASSE IN BOW GLACIER, 1910

Crevasses are cracks in the upper surface of a glacier caused by the ice flowing over irregularities in the bedrock. The 1910 trip to Yoho Glacier and across the Continental Divide to Bow Glacier was an opportunity for glacial studies by A.O.Wheeler and photography by Byron Harmon.

AN ICE CAVE IN YOHO GLACIER, 1910

Ice caves are mysterious and enchanting places hollowed out in glaciers by summer meltwater. This photograph is half of a stereo negative. Ice caves are good subjects for the illusion of depth created by stereo photographs.

271. A DAYS HUNT. THREE GRIZZLIES.

A.O. WHEELER AND TOM LONGSTAFF WITH THREE GRIZZLY BEAR CARCASSES, 1910

Hunting for food and trophies and trapping were accepted in the early days in the Rockies. This photograph was taken at the head of the Howser Valley in the Purcell Mountains.

TOM LONGSTAFF, BERT BARROW, AND CHARLES LAWRENCE DRESSING GRIZZLY BEAR HIDES, 1910

The ACC reconnaissance of the Spillamacheen Spires (Bugaboos) in the Purcell Range, also included A.O. Wheeler, Conrad Kain, and Byron Harmon.

AROUND THE CAMPFIRE IN THE PURCELL MOUNTAINS, 1910

A.O.Wheeler, Tom Longstaff, Conrad Kain, Charles Lawrence, Bert Barrow, and Byron Harmon relax around the campfire.

MARMOLOTA, PIGEON, AND SNOWPATCH SPIRES, AND BUGABOO GLACIER, 1910

Bugaboo Glacier, discovered by Byron Harmon in 1910, was originally called Great Harmon Glacier. A gold claim staked near Bugaboo Pass in 1895 turned out to be mainly pyrite and galena.

BYRON HARMON IN CAMP, YELLOWHEAD EXPEDITION, 1911

In 1911 one of the most ambitious expeditions ever undertaken in the Rockies was organized by the ACC. The expedition started in Banff, travelled north to the Columbia Icefield and Maligne Lake; then west to Yellowhead Pass, circumnavigating Mt. Robson; and then returning to Banff through early autumn snows.

CHARLES WALCOTT, JR., WITH A CARIBOU HEAD,
1911

The intention of the Yellowhead Expedition was to collect as much scientific information about the region as possible. Failing to interest Canadian scientists in the endeavor, A.O.Wheeler approached Charles Walcott, Jr., Secretary of the Smithsonian Institution and won his enthusiastic support. Ned Hollister, R.H.Riley, Charles Walcott, Jr., and Henry Blagden represented the Smithsonian on the trip. This caribou head was one of the specimens collected during the expedition.

PANORAMA VIEW OF MT. ROBSON, 1911

The highest peak is Mt. Robson, towering above Berg Lake and Berg Glacier. The Robson Glacier is on the left. This is one of the very few panorama views by Byron Harmon.

CAMP ABOVE EMPEROR FALLS AT MT. ROBSON, 1911

The campfire was not just a pleasant place to sit. Camp life included: mending clothes, repairing equipment, drying boots and socks, and preparing elaborate meals of stew, bannock, etc.

MT. ROBSON FROM THE EAST, 1911 OR 1913

Today the east face of Mt. Robson is still relatively inaccessible, seen only by a few climbers and hardy back-packers who are willing to circum-navigate the mountain. Mt. Robson is the highest peak in the Canadian Rockies at 3954 m. The first significant attempt to climb Mt. Robson occured in 1909. Curly Phillips, an Ontario trapper and canoe guide, arrived in the Rockies, and he encountered George Kinney on his way north to attempt a solo ascent of Mt. Robson. Although Phillips had never been on a mountain in his life, he joined Kinney and the two did succeed in reaching the summit of Robson in a whiteout. Credit for the first ascent should have been theirs, but in the whiteout they left their marker somewhat below the summit. (See p. 44.)

PHIMISTER PROCTOR PAINTING AT MALIGNE LAKE, 1911

Phimister Proctor was an American artist from New York. In those days, when landscape painting was still popular, it was common for artists to journey into the wilderness in search of exciting subjects in nature.

WAITING FOR THE LIGHT, 1911

Unnamed companion and Byron Harmon wait for the lighting at Amethyst Lake, with Moat Lake and The Ramparts in the distance. Is this a photograph by an unidentified person or a self-portrait set up and directed by Byron Harmon himself?

SUMMIT CITY, YELLOWHEAD PASS, 1911

"... make-shift stores, rough log buildings with canvas roofs, as many billiard and soft drink saloons, a railway contractor's camp and a blacksmith shop ... a "shooting" the night we were there but no one seems to have been hurt."
A.O. Wheeler, *Canadian Alpine Journal*, 1912

LEWIS SWIFT'S FLOUR MILL, 1911

Lewis Swift ranched and traded with the Métis in the area. When Jasper National Park was established in 1910 Swift refused to sell to the government. Later he sold to a dude ranch operator. The national park eventually bought the land in 1962.

CURLY PHILLIPS AND REV. GEORGE KINNEY IN CAMP, 1911

These men made the first serious attempt on Mt. Robson in 1909. (See p. 41.)

PACK TRAIN ON THE UPPER SUNWAPTA RIVER, 1911

The Yellowhead Expedition returned to Banff through early autumn snow. This makes for picturesque but difficult travelling for the horses.

JOHN HUNTER PREPARING FOR THE SUN DANCE

The Sun Dance is one of the most sacred and secret of Native initiation ceremonies. At one time it was outlawed by the Canadian government, so photographs of this ceremony are rare. There was once a complete series of Byron Harmon photographs of this ceremony. All but two negatives were subsequently lost or destroyed.

THE SUMMIT OF MT. RESPLENDENT, 1913

In 1913 The ACC sent a party of climbers to Mt. Robson to finally conquer the elusive summit that many parties had tried, and failed to capture. A number of adjacent peaks were also climbed including neighboring Mt. Resplendent.

CONRAD KAIN ON THE GENDARME OF MT. RESPLENDENT, 1913

Mt. Resplendent was first climbed by Conrad Kain and Byron Harmon in 1911 during the Yellowhead Pass Expedition. Kain led several parties of the ACC to the summit in 1913.

CLIMBERS FROM
THE MT. ROBSON
ACC CAMP ON
AN UNIDENTIFIED
GLACIER,
1913
Mt. Robson is
flanked with
formidable
glaciers that make
the summit all the
more tantalizing
and difficult to
reach.

CONRAD KAIN, ALBERT MACCARTHY, AND WILLIAM FOSTER, 1913

This photograph was taken after the first recognized ascent of Mt. Robson. Conrad Kain led the party using a route he had worked out when observing the mountain in 1911.

CLIMBERS ON AN UNIDENTIFIED GLACIER, 1913

This photograph of a party from the ACC camp at Mt. Robson illustrates the planning that Byron Harmon put into his photography.

A CREVASSE NEAR MT. ROBSON, 1913

This is another of Byron Harmon's posed shots intended to illustrate as well as to amuse. Crevasses in the Rockies may be up to 40 metres deep and on the upper reaches of a glacier they may be covered with snow. A fall in a crevasse can be fatal.

295. ICE CREVASSE.

AN ICE CAVE AT THE OUTLET OF ROBSON GLACIER, 1913

This party of four climbers from the 1913 ACC camp at Mt. Robson appear in a number of photographs.

Who are they? Perhaps they are Dr. Stone, Miss Broadbent, Mr. Frind, and Mr. Conrad Kain who made the second ascent of Mt. Resplendent.

BYRON HARMON Byron may have dressed up in the cowboy outfit for this self-portrait. His son and daughter claim he never dressed this way.

MRS. PETER EAR

ISAAC
ROLLINGMUD

JONAS GOODSTONEY

PARADE AT BANFF INDIAN DAYS, CA 1912

In 1889 torrential rains washed out the CPR tracks, stranding guests at the Banff Springs Hotel. Tom Wilson arranged for the Stoneys to demonstrate dances, beginning the anuual Banff Indian Days. They continued until 1978.

CHRISTIAN HÄSLER, JR., UNIDENTIFIED BOY, AND ERNEST FEUZ ON MT. MCGILL

Mt. McGill is located in the upper Cougar Valley in the Selkirk Range, Mt. Sir Donald is seen in the distance. Christian Häsler and Ernest Feuz were two of the renowned Swiss guides brought to the Rockies by the CPR to guide guests during the summer seasons. A number of these guides remained in Canada, settling near Golden, BC.

ROCK CLIMBING

Mountain climbing has changed dramatically since the turn of the century. Then, with few first ascents made, the object was to reach the summit, usually by the easiest route. Approaches to the mountain were much longer and more difficult. Today, with no remaining first ascents to make, attention has turned to technical climbing and conquering difficult routes.

SERACS ON THE ILLECILLEWAET GLACIER

Seracs are pillars of ice that form in icefalls on glaciers or along the cliff edge of hanging glaciers. They are among the most picturesque of glacial features, but are avoided in glacial travel.

BYRON HARMON AT A GLACIAL LAKE IN THE SELKIRK RANGE

This glacial lake was located between Mt. Sir Donald and Mt. Macoum at the edge of the Illecillewaet Glacier. The photograph is likely a self-portrait.

NEAR ASULKAN PASS WITH MT. DAWSON AND DAWSON GLACIER BEYOND

The Swiss guides in this photograph are Christian Häsler, Jr., an unidentified guide, and Ernest Feuz. The peaks of Mt. Dawson are in the background from left to right: Feuz, Häsler, and Michel peaks, named after Swiss guides.

BYRON HARMON WITH HIS MOVIE CAMERA OVERLOOKING ILLECILLEWAET VALLEY

The Selkirk Mountains are more rugged and steeper than the Rockies. They have been a favourite with climbers since before the turn of the century.

CLIMBERS ON A MORAINE NEAR YOHO GLACIER, 1914

The climbers are from the ACC camp in upper Yoho Valley. Yoho Glacier has receded greatly throughout this century. It is now very difficult to find the exact location of this photograph.

CLIMBERS ON YOHO GLACIER, 1914

Yoho Glacier flows out of the Wapta Icefield on the Continental Divide. The other side of the icefield descends in the Bow Glacier, Peyto Glacier, and other glaciers seen from the Icefield Parkway.

AN ICE CAVE IN ATHABASCA GLACIER, 1914

About this time, Byron Harmon made a feature length film about travelling north to the Columbia Icefield and Mt. Robson. He sold it to Associated Screen News before 1917. But today the where-abouts of virtually all the Harmon movie footage is unknown.

ON BOW GLACIER, 1917

Seracs and crevasses surround this climber on Bow Glacier.

CROWFOOT GLACIER, 1914 OR 1917

The packtrain is on what is now the trail to Helen Lake. Crowfoot Glacier was most certainly named for its appearance. The lower claw fell off in one enormous avalanche that was reportedly heard in Lake Louise many miles south.

HORSES IN A SMUDGE, 1917

Were mosquitoes and flies more bothersome in the old days than now? Likely they were from written accounts of their torments. Smudge fires were sometimes built to drive them off and the horses would crowd into the protecting smoke.

BASTION PEAK, TURRET MOUNTAIN, AND MT. GEIKIE, 1918

Mt. Geikie and The Ramparts are located in Tonquin Valley near Jasper. Mt. Geikie was named after a famous geologist, Sir Archibald Geikie, Director-General of the Geological Survey of Great Britain from 1882 to 1901.

A LOCOMOTIVE ENTERING THE SPIRAL TUNNELS, MT. STEPHEN ABOVE
The Spiral Tunnels were built within Mt. Ogden and Cathedral Mountain to reduce the grade of "the Big Hill" near Field, BC. Over a thousand men were employed for two years constructing the two tunnels.

A ROOM IN THE BANFF SPRINGS HOTEL

On opening in 1888, the Banff Springs Hotel was the largest in the world. CPR Vice-President William Cornelius Van Horne selected the site. He envisioned a series of hotels and thousands of tourists flocking to them on CPR trains.

THE LOBBY OF THE BANFF SPRINGS HOTEL

While peaks were being climbed and new country explored, the civilized centres were expanding at a rapid rate. The Banff Springs Hotel was world-renowned by early in the twentieth century. Its guest register included guests from Europe, North America, and Asia.

TEAHOUSE AT LAKE AGNES, 1923

The teahouse at Lake Agnes was built in 1905 by the CPR and is still in operation in a reconstructed building under private management. Perched directly above Bridal Veil Falls on the shore of Lake Agnes, it is one of the most picturesque spots in the Rockies.

DON HARMON FEEDING A DEER, CA1920

Wildlife and people have lived in proximity since Banff was established. Elk and deer roam the streets and bears are occasionally seen on the outskirts. Don Harmon, Byron's son, took over the photographic business after World War II.

A MAN STANDING IN A FLOCK OF PELICANS, 1920

Byron Harmon photographed wildlife far less than he photographed mountains or people. His wildlife photographs often have a humorous twist to them that is charming.

A SNOWSHOER ABOVE JOHNSTON CANYON, PILOT MOUNTAIN IN THE DISTANCE

Before skiing was introduced to the Rockies in the late 1920s snowshoes and dog team were the only forms of winter travel. Snowshoes are better than skis in the forest and were used extensively in the Rockies by trappers and guides.

NEAR JUMBO CREEK, 1920

Byron Harmon's movie trip to the Lake of the Hanging Glaciers included plans to shoot a film about goat hunting. This involved Conrad Kain shooting a goat in advance and relocating it to a scenic spot for the making of the film.

DR. CORA JOHNSTONE BEST, MRS. "CHERE" SHIPPHAM, AND MR. CONRAD KAIN, 1922

Following the 1922 ACC camp Conrad Kain guided Cora Best and Chere Shippham to the Lake of the Hanging Glaciers, accompanied by Byron Harmon.

THE LAKE OF THE HANGING GLACIERS, 1922

In his editorial notes in Conrad Kain's autobiography, J. Monroe Thorington comments on this trip, "One would like to know the whole story of that excursion in the Purcells, for rumor will have it that Mrs. Best carried a revolver and pointed it on occasion. But the lady is no longer with us and Conrad and Harmon will never tell." *Where the Clouds Can Go.* (See also Cora Best's account in the *Canadian Alpine Journal,* 1923.)

THE LAKE OF THE HANGING GLACIERS WITH MT. SERGEANT AND MT. LIEUTENANT AT CENTRE, 1920

Byron Harmon visited The Lake of the Hanging Glaciers to make movies in 1920 and 1922. Both times he encountered American writer and film-maker Lewis Freeman.

ICE CAVE IN STARBIRD GLACIER, 1922

Originally known as Horsethief Glacier, Cora Best, Chere Shippham, and Conrad Kain are on the ice promontory. "The big cave is all of three hundred yards long. Its arched dome, where winds have kept a constant melting process going on, is polished jade-green." (Cora Best, *Canadian Alpine Journal,* 1923.)

SCOTTY WRIGHT, 1920

Scotty Wright was a game warden. This and the following picture are labelled in the negative collection as Ptarmigan Pass hunting trip.

SCOTTY WRIGHT, 1920

This pair of photographs may be the quintessential example of Byron Harmon's quirky sense of humour.

BYRON HARMON PHOTOGRAPHING IN THE KANANASKIS VALLEY

Is this one of a series of photographs taken over the years by Byron Harmon of photographing in difficult places? In many of these photographs the scene toward which the camera is pointed is less interesting than the picture of the photographer.

A PARTY OF FISHERMEN IN THE KANANASKIS VALLEY

At the time this picture was probably taken, it is unlikely this fishing party would have gone to the trouble of erecting a teepee. More likely, this is one of Byron Harmon's teepee shots, staged for the camera.

LAKE LOUISE TRAMLINE, CA 1920

A narrow guage tramline took guests bound for Chateau Lake Louise up the long hill from Laggan Station to the hotel. The tramline was built in 1913 and abandoned in 1930 when a road was built to the Chateau.

GATEWAY TO ROCKY MOUNTAINS PARK, 1921

In 1885, Banff Hot Springs Reserve was established, an area of ten square miles. In June 1887 the name was changed to Rocky Mountains Park and the area was expanded to the foothills beyond Devils Gap.

SINCLAIR CANYON, 1923

The Banff-Windermere Road, now Highway 93, was officially opened in 1923. Byron Harmon lost no time in taking advantage of the opportunity provided by the road to organize a canoe trip on the Kootenay River.

CANOEING ON THE CROSS RIVER, 1923

The Cross River is a subsidiary of the Kootenay River. This photograph is from a series of images that show canoeing and the canoe capsizing. Perhaps this is another example of the story-telling theme so evident in Byron Harmon's photography.

A KOOTENAY
NATIVE WOMAN
AND CHILD,
1923

CROSSING SASKATCHEWAN GLACIER, 1924

In 1924 Byron Harmon teamed up with Lewis Freeman to make a movie of a packtrain trip from Banff to Jasper. The Columbia Icefield Expedition resulted in not only the movie but a book, *On the Roof of the Rockies,* and a major article in *National Geographic* magazine. Harmon's attitude to competition in film-making is quoted in Freeman's book, *Down the Columbia.* "There's room for a hundred cameramen up there, and the more the world is shown of the wonders of the Rockies and Selkirks, the more it will want to see. It will be good to have your company, and each of us ought to be of help to the other."

BOW LAKE, 1924

Everything about the Columbia Icefield Expedition was staged for the camera, even if it meant a more inconvenient or dangerous route. In this photograph of Bow Lake the teepee is pitched in a marshy area where one would never choose to camp. This scene was so popular that other local photographers copied it, setting up a teepee in the same place each summer for visitors to photograph. On this expedition Byron Harmon had a stereo camera along, as well as his motion picture camera, 5x7 view camera, and a smaller view camera.

BOB BAPTIE ON THE SUMMIT OF MT. CASTLEGUARD, 1924

Bob Baptie was one of the cowboys along on the Columbia Icefield Expedition. The other members of the party were Soapy Smith and Ulysse La Casse who was the cook. Mt. Castleguard is one of the peaks on the southern end of the Columbia Icefield.

THE TOE OF SASKATCHEWAN GLACIER, 1924

Stereo photographs are made by a camera with two lenses separated by the distance between the eyes. When viewed with a stereo viewer the brain recreates the illusion of depth of the original scene.

MT. SASKATCHEWAN FROM MT. CASTLEGUARD, 1924

Byron Harmon used a stereo camera on the Columbia Icefield Expedition. He chose subjects wisely. The great depth of field from foreground to background enhances the stereo (3-D) effect.

BYRON HARMON IN CASTLEGUARD CAVE, 1924

Castleguard Cave is the entrance to an extensive cave system beneath the Columbia Icefield. The cave is prone to sudden flooding, and access is restricted.

MT. BRYCE FROM THE COLUMBIA ICEFIELD, 1924

Mt. Bryce was named by Norman Collie for Lord James Bryce, jurist, historian, alpinist, diplomat, and President of the Alpine Club in England.

BOB BAPTIE AND SOAPY SMITH LISTENING TO THE WIRELESS RADIO, 1924

Byron Harmon and Lewis Freeman were remarkably alike in spirit and imagination. Unusual additions to the baggage on this expedition were a wireless radio contributed by Freeman, and carrier pigeons contributed by Harmon, as well as a portable typewriter to type messages on oiled paper. The radio underwent severe trials in stream crossings, but they listened to the news from Vancouver and Oakland, California.

SOAPY SMITH AND LEWIS FREEMAN LISTENING TO THE RADIO AT SASKATCHEWAN GLACIER, 1924

The adventurers listen to a message sent from Banff to Oakland by carrier pigeon and read out on the Oakland radio station. The expedition's own carrier pigeons never reached Banff.

PACK HORSES ON SASKATCH-EWAN GLACIER, 1924

Most earlier expeditions bypassed the Columbia Icefield by way of Wilcox Pass. The idea of crossing the Icefield had been tried in 1923 by a mountaineering party. It was a hazardous plan and arduous for the horses but made for great photographs.

SOAPY SMITH FORDING THE CHABA RIVER WITH DRAGON PEAK IN THE BACKGROUND

River crossings were inevitable in the early days of mountain travel. Mountain streams are swift and freezing cold as they roar down from the glaciers. It was not unusual for horses to lose their footing or for swimming horses to be swept downstream with calamitous results to the food, bedding, or camera supplies they carried. Soapy Smith was in charge of the horses for the trip.

MT. QUINCY, 1924

Mt. Quincy was named by Lucius Quincy Coleman, a rancher at Morley, Alberta for his mothers family. He accompanied his brother, A.P. Coleman, a geologist from Toronto, on many trips in the mountains. A.P. Coleman wrote an entertaining book on his early explorations in the Canadian Rockies: *The Canadian Rockies, New and Old Trails,* 1911.

MT. COLUMBIA, 1924

At Byron's insistence, the expedition waited in camp through eight days of snow and cloud to get this picture of Mt. Columbia. Lewis Freeman describes their triumph in *On the Roof of the Rockies*: "Then, suddenly and without warning, the veiling clouds fell away like a parted curtain. ...The view lasted for forty minutes, ever changing but ever beautiful, and in that time we exposed still negatives at the rate of one a minute, besides running 400 feet of motion picture film. The black rectangles of paper from Harmon's film packs were piled up behind his tripods like the brass shells around a hard-pumped machine-gun at the end of a battle."

MALIGNE LAKE, 1924

Beautiful Maligne Lake, east of Jasper, was the northernmost extent of this expedition. It returned south to Banff through early snowfalls in the high passes. This was planned by Harmon for the dramatic photographic opportunities that would be encountered.

ULYSSE LA CASSE ASSISTING PACK HORSES, 1924

Ulysse La Casse was the cook on this expedition but he was also an experienced horse wrangler. In 1931 he became a park warden. His good nature and sense of humor made him a popular companion on the trail.

ASCENDING THE DIVIDE BETWEEN POBOKTAN AND JONAS CREEKS, 1924

Lewis Freeman describes the trip home to Banff, begun on October 7 and finished on October 24, in an article for *National Geographic*, "For the next ten days, save for wind-swept peaks and small patches under thick trees, we never saw the bare earth. In the lower valleys snow was from six inches to two feet in depth; on the passes and in drifted ravines we broke our way through from four to six feet. Our hardest fights were over the divide between Poboktan and Jonas creeks, and at the pass between the Brazeau and the Cline."

ELSIE BROOKS
FEEDING A BEAR

Elsie Brooks was an employee of Byron Harmon for a number of years. Feeding the bears was a common entertainment until very recently when Parks Canada radically tightened its policies on garbage control and on visitor education.

759. ON BANFF-WINDERMERE ROAD.

RCMP OFFICER AND BEAR

The foibles of bears in camp, bears in town, and bears along the highways offered rich fodder for Byron Harmon and his camera. This photograph was no doubt staged although the mounties did not retire their red uniforms from everyday attire until the 1960s.

The Sore Horsemen

of the Apocalypse

JOHN MURRAY GIBBON

Gibbon was an author and publicist for the CPR, avidly promoting the Rockies through art and photography. Byron Harmon took him on a packtrip through the Rockies including Kootenay Park and the Goodsirs.

MT. GOODSIR FROM THE SOUTHEAST

This photograph shows the South Tower of Mt. Goodsir at centre. Teepee Peak is to the left of the Lyall's larch tree.

UNIDENTIFIED MAN BESIDE A SNOW MUSHROOM IN GLACIER PARK, 1925

Being west of the Continental Divide, Glacier National Park experiences much heavier snowfall than do the eastern slopes of the Rockies. Fantastic snow sculptures form on trees and bushes. In this photograph the man is standing in a hollow around the trunk of the buried tree stump.

THREE SKIERS NEAR GLACIER HOUSE, 1921

Edward Feuz, an unidentified man, and Christian Häsler, Jr., pose for this photograph. Edward and Ernest Feuz and Christian Häsler are Swiss guides who appear in many of Byron Harmon's photographs.

SHOVELLING SNOW OFF THE ROOF OF GLACIER HOUSE, 1925

Glacier House was the first hotel built by the CPR located in Rogers Pass near the Illecillewaet Glacier.

FRED PEPPER AND HIS DOGTEAM, 1925

Fred Pepper was a guide who lived in Field, BC. This trip included photographs of dog sledding as well as marvellous scenic photographs of snow formations.

BYRON HARMON WITH MOTION PICTURE CAMERA AND SNOWSHOES, 1925

His children claim that Byron Harmon didn't ski, although there are pictures of him on skis beside the Bow River. Probably, like many of the trappers and guides, he was more comfortable on snowshoes than on the new-fangled skis, which were becoming popular in the 1920s. Jimmy Simpson, a crusty old guide, referred to skiers as, "people with wooden heads and feet to match."

BANFF AVENUE, 1925

Cascade Mountain towering above Banff Avenue may be the most photographed scene in the Canadian Rockies. Through the years we have seen it as a dirt road with cows on it, with deer crossing it, and during countless parades. Thousands of tourists have posed here.

BANFF AVENUE DURING BANFF WINTER CARNIVAL, 1929

The first Banff Winter Carnival was held in 1917. An ice palace of ice blocks was built by prisoners of war interned in Banff. The ice sculptures were carved by local sculptor Charlie Beil; teepees were the contribution of the Stoneys.

INTERIOR OF HARMONY DRUGSTORE, "THE STORE WITH THE PICTURES"
Byron Harmon was an entrepreneur as well as a wilderness photographer. He built a movie house that burned down in 1917, followed by a large store organized rather like a tiny department store that included a drugstore and assorted other services throughout the years. But there were always pictures, on every surface which could be utilized, and in every size imaginable.

A STONEY WITH A HORSE AND TRAVOIS

The travois was an ingenious device used by Natives to transport heavy loads.

A STONEY DRESSING AN ANIMAL SKIN

MT. ASSINIBOINE, 1927

Mt. Assiniboine is one of the highest peaks in the Rockies, located in Mt. Assiniboine Provincial Park, adjoining Banff National Park. The beautiful valley around Mt. Assiniboine is one of the most popular hiking areas in the Rockies. In earlier years, before Canada had established its own identity, Assiniboine was called the Matterhorn of the Canadian Alps.

HELEN BREESE WALCOTT AT MT. ASSINIBOINE, 1927

The ACC camp was held in the Assiniboine Valley in 1927. One of the guests was Helen Breese Walcott, daughter of Dr.Charles Walcott, Secretary of the Smithsonian Institution. He spent many summers in the Rockies and discovered the fossils in the Burgess Shale, now a World Heritage Site, and one of the most unique fossil beds in the world.

IKE MILLS, 1932

A porcupine's quills are loosely attached to its coat and come loose at the slightest touch, embedding their barbed ends in the victim's body. Dogs are often the unwitting recipient of their favours and there is no choice but to remove the quills one by one with pliers.

IKE MILLS AT SKOKI, 1932

Ike Mills and his dogteam were in demand in the winter when horses could not be used to pack supplies into the newly built ski lodges at Skoki and Mt. Assiniboine.

SKIERS AT SKOKI, 1932

Skoki Lodge near Lake Louise was the first back-country ski lodge built in the Canadian Rockies. It was built by a group of local ski enthusiasts and opened its doors for the winter season of 1931.

SKIERS AT MT. NORQUAY, 1932

It was a natural development for skiers to want to travel faster and tackle steeper slopes. Before lifts were constructed enthusiasts would walk for miles to get to the alpine slopes, climbing up the steep hills for a thrilling ride down.

MR. AND MRS.
BEN KAQUITTS

MRS. JOB
BEAVER
AT AGE 102,
1934

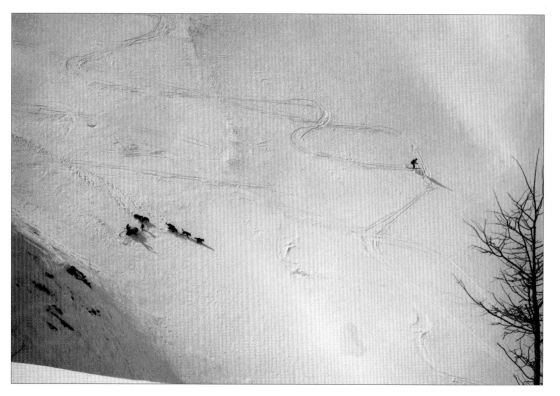

IKE MILLS DOGTEAM AND A LONE SKIER NEAR MT. ASSINIBOINE, 1934

Mt. Assiniboine camp was purchased by Ehrling Strom and the Marquis delgi Albizzi in 1928 to use as a ski camp, the beginning of back-country skiing in the Rockies.

IKE MILLS WITH THE TOWERS AND NAISET PEAK, 1934

The Assiniboine Valley is a marvellous area for skiing with great snow and a variety of terrain.

AILEEN HARMON AND MT. ASSINIBOINE, 1934

Aileen Harmon followed in her father's footsteps in her love of mountain travel and adventure. She became the first naturalist with Parks Canada in Banff National Park and pioneered many of the nature trails that are still used as interpretive walks today.

MT. MAGOG AND MT. ASSINIBOINE, 1934

Mt. Assiniboine was named for the Stoney custom of cooking food by plunging hot rocks into containers of liquid to raise the temperature.

A DIVER POISED OVER VICTORIA GLACIER, CA 1932
Until the 1980s the Chateau Lake Louise had a beautiful swimming pool in the spacious grounds beside the lake. The structure is still there but the pool has been replaced by an indoor pool to serve guests year round.